IDENTITY IN CHRIST

JOHANNES TEFO

Identity In Christ

Johannes Tefo

Published by Johannes Tefo, 2024.

Also by Johannes Tefo

Family spiritual Warfare Books
Youth's Guide To Spiritual Warfare
A Women's Guide To Spiritual Warfare

Standalone
Deliver Your Soul From Evil: Self Deliverance Guide
Deliverance From Mind Control: Be Free And Delivered From
Every Marine Demons Of Mind Control
Overcoming Spirit Of Stagnation
The 24: Prophetic Word For This Season 2024 And Beyond
Michael For Warfare
Territorial Spirits: Overcome Evil Strongholds in Your Life And
Take Over Your Community With Strategic Warfare And Win-
ning Prayers
Prayers Against Suicide Spirit
Spiritual Warfare When Enough is Enough
Identity In Christ

Table of Contents

Who art thou? 1

Assignment, Office, and the Name. 7

Seeing yourself in light of Scriptures. 15

5 ways of Seeing Yourself in the Scriptures. 19

Who you identify you, influences you. 21

Identity Crisis. 25

Identity in Christ. | Chosen before Creation. 27

We are the children of God. 30

We are new Creation. 32

Heirs of God and Co-heirs with Christ. 34

Chosen People, Royal Priesthood, and God's special possession. 36

A Royal Priesthood: 37

A Holy Nation: 38

God's Special Possession: 39

Called Out of Darkness into Light: 40

I am sanctified and Justified. 41

Nothing can separate me from the Love of God. 43

Fearfully and wonderfully made. 45

Rescued from dominion of darkness. 47

Christ lives in me. 49

In Christ 100 Prayer Points | 100 prayer points inspired by the identity we have in Christ: 51

100 prayer points inspired by Psalms, reflecting on the identity we have in Christ: 58

100 prayer points inspired by the prophetic books from Daniel to Malachi: 65

In Christ 100 prayer points based on the New Testament. ... 76

I dedicate this book to friends and family in Christ all over the world. Let the spirit of Christ reign in your hearts.

This is a deep question. Who art though? And many of us tend to conclude what we like and don't like to make up our persona. We base this answer according to our personality and identity imputed by external factors. And in most cases, personality is built up by external factors. The music we listen to, clothes we wear, careers we chose, the circle of friends we hang out with, and so on.

This is the same question the Pharisees sent their soldiers to ask John the Baptist "Who art thou"? since John knew who he was, he answered them in the light of the scriptures *"I am The voice of one crying in the wilderness, Prepare ye the way of the Lord, make his paths straight"*.

The purpose and destiny of John was revealed by the hand of angels. It goes to say, if you want to know who you are, allow the Holy Spirit to reveal who you are. John found himself when he read Isaiah 40:3. Jesus Christ found himself in the scripture Isaiah 61:1. It is in light of the Word of God that mirrors our purpose and destinies in life. When we look deep within ourselves enough, we can come out with a fully verged testimony of who we are.

While many go around this world looking for validation from the outside world—we look within where lies the endless possibilities. Holy Spirit is your friend. God left a holy mark in our hearts so that we can bear witness to His goodness. John the Baptist was filled with the Holy Ghost even before birth.

The spirit of power in the life of John sustained him and molded him into the great man of God he was. Christ holds John above all prophets who ever lived. It is the spirit of humility, grace, and power that earned John the prestige as the last great prophet of the bible. But there would not be John if there was not Elijah. The prophetic line of Elijah to Elisha, and lastly to John, is the prophetic office of power that concerns itself with righteousness and holiness.

John did not look at his physical appearance, or rather, allow the external factor to dictate who he was. The greatest shift in his life happened when he broke away from the normal tradition of staying in the synagogue of that time, or Jerusalem for the service of priesthood. He went to the wilderness and encountered the Most High. If he had to comfortably enjoy the priestly benefits of being a Levi in the temple of Jerusalem, he would have never realized his calling.

Like many of us, we living other people's calling. We are validated by others, neglecting our core values and God-given dreams that we should have embarked on years ago—taking the less road traveled.

God is looking for those who will allow the Holy Spirit to mold them into who they are supposed to be.

Psalm 100:3 Know ye that the LORD he is God: it is he that hath made us, and not we
ourselves; we are his people, and the sheep of his pasture.

Knowing the fact that we come from the Lord will save us from many troubles and direct our life paths according to the roots we stem from. God is spirit. The spirit part of ourselves is as important as much as we care about the body. Spirit keeps the body going. If you can know the fullness of your spirit, you will know that you are capable of anything.

We know that we can do anything through Christ. We also learn about the importance of words; that words are spirit. Words, thoughts, and imaginations are powerhouse you have to direct your path in line with the destiny of God. In Christ, we have the mind of Christ. The spirit man is the real man. Nourishing the real man within, you shall see the power of God and His grace abounds in your life.

Apostle Peter knew himself as the rock after an encounter with Christ. This is what we call life destiny. Fishermen we turned into fishers of men. We can also look at the greatest Apostle, Paul, it was only after an encounter with Jesus Christ that he knew his lifetime mission—taking the gospel of Jesus Christ to the world. When you come to God, He reveals who you are. You do not have to waste time looking at who you are outside of the Godhead.

God is first and foremost. Education cannot give you a godly identity. A good paying job will not also help you find yourself. You first understand that you are a spirit. And as a spirit, your hungry spirit needs to be fed with spiritual food to fully function to the best of your ability. God is that energy source to give light to your spirit man. Christ is the way, truth, and life you will ever need.

You start to learn that you were born with the spirit of power. Here is what the Psalmist had to say,

Psalm 8:2 Out of the mouth of babes and sucklings hast thou or-
dained strength
because of thine enemies, that thou mightest still the enemy and the
avenger.

How much more do we need when even out of the mouth of babes comes power? Children of God are ordained with the power to silence the works of the darkness. We have Christ who has triumphed over ancient powers of evil that have been holding us hostage for so long.

Let us be for Christ. We are living in difficult times whereby media is slowly destroying the real identity of men and women. We are buying into this worldly culture that is destroying our souls every day. The real success is determined by how your Instagram page looks, or how much following you have on overall social media. While in the background folks are depressed and suicidal in keeping up with the social demands. God help us!

Identity issues are what keeps many from taking action—reaching their destinies. The life of John the Baptist was revealed by Angel Gabriel to his parents; the name, office, and his function. I also believe that his parents played a huge role in his identity. The fact that in due time, he left his native to lodge in the wilderness, was a testament to the spirit of Elijah at play at that point.

The family has a role to play in our call of God. We see in the life of Abraham, that God called him out of his native for a different path. God wanted to have a special relationship with Abraham, and He wouldn't in Haran because of its idolatry. Before He could have a serious walk with Gideon, God told him to destroy the idol of his father's house; altars of Baal and Ashtoreth.

You will have to lose something to gain Christ. Peter lost His fisherman job. Many have lost their family for following Christ. Even some, have lost their lives for the call of Christ. Christ is worth more than gold and diamonds combined. Christ's treasures are eternal. You cannot miss eternal bliss for temporal enjoyment. Folks, we can still enjoy what life has to offer even in the house of prayer. The kingdom of God is the government of prayer.

Parents in the Lord can get you so far in the things of the Lord. Like Samuel, you have to stand up on your own and be your generation. Priest Eli can teach you about the ways of the Lord but the future lies in your hands to inspire your generation.

Moses was the greatest prophet who ever lived but there came a time when he had to live this earth. Joshua was the man to be ordained into the prophetic office of Moses, the man of God. Joshua had to be strong, man up, and lead his generation through faith. While people are not replaceable, through faith, men and women can do valiant things.

While you might be submitting under a certain ministry, it is also a good thing to develop your faith and relationship with your God in a secret place. Your altar in the secret place will sustain you. No man can sustain you but the spirit of the Living God. This goes to my African brothers and sisters in the Lord. It all comes down to identity in the Lord. Do what God has called you to do, not what your Pastor calls you to do. Humility is great but only under the leadership of the Holy Spirit.

It does not do good to respect the culture we are in while neglecting the mighty God, who is above all, and in all.

Psalm 82:6 I have said, Ye are gods; and all of you are children of the most High.

Scripture cannot be broken. This scripture says "Ye are gods". The spirit in you is Holy as it is the breath from the Holy mouth of the Holy Father. You are the child of the Most High God. This is the identity you bear, and it will never change. This is your first DNA.

We also draw power from the blood of Christ. While other pagan religions strengthen themselves with the blood of animals, we pride ourselves on the precious blood of the lamb as the real testament of victory over our lives. God is great folks!

See yourself how God sees you. See yourself in Christ. See yourself complete. Walking in the perfection of Christ through faith. It can only be through the faith of Abraham that we can please God. Life is great when you are all about pleasing God rather than men. You cannot please men and win this race called life. Take heart. Be courageous like Joshua.

Assignment, Office, and the Name.

Psalm 68:18 Thou hast ascended on high, thou hast led captivity
captive: thou hast
received gifts for men; yea, for the rebellious also, that the LORD
God might
dwell among them.

Jesus Christ granted men gifts when he ascended. He first descended to the lower parts of the earth to lead the captivity captive. The renowned men and women of faith who died in the Lord. Before Christ, the dead saints in the Lord never went to heaven but to Paradise which was located in the lower parts. This was the abode of Abraham. Note that, Abraham's promises from the Lord extend even beyond physical land. He inherited also spiritual land. This is the man who was looking for a city not built by humans but by God himself.

The death of Christ brought not only salvation on earth but brought together redemption even unto the deceased saints of old. Death lost its grip on power through the blood of the lamb. The blood of Christ is spiritual, in the eyes of the spirit, the blood is the light of God. Someone covered by the blood of Christ, in the spirit realm is adorned by the light of glory. You should never in any way compromise your light to fit in this culture. Light drives out darkness.

As the body of Christ, the church, we ought to discern the body of Christ. His body was holy. His body was clothed in a godly manner. His body was dedicated unto the Lord to servitude of holiness and righteousness. His body was the house of prayer, the temple of the holy spirit. finally, His body was broken for our sake—the death of the Cross!

The death to self is the new life of the spirit in Christ. Through the body of Christ, we can live the life God wants. The life of faith, hope, and love—looking unto Christ the perfection of our souls. The office and assignments of our calling come from the Lord. There comes trouble when your gift is alienated from the Lord. When you no longer abide in the secret place of God. You will start seeing brothers and sisters in the Lord and start forcing prophecies, sermons, teachings, etc.

When you take a fish out of the sea, it is bound to die. The same applies when you drift away from God, the fire in your soul dries out. In the Tabernacle, Moses was commanded to keep the lights burning. The lights in the temple were not supposed to dim off. We are also the house of prayer. Let the fire keep burning till we meet Christ.

The calling we have is the calling of fire. The kingdom of power in words and deeds. This is the dimension Christ walked in—the dimension of the spirit of power and glory. After the forty-day fast, He returned with the power of spirit. He taught in authority. He preached in Authority. He did start in power and finished in power. The principle of prayer and fasting was part of the lifestyle of Christ. Even the Apostle after Christ, still applied the principles of prayer and fasting.

Ephesians 2:20 Now therefore ye are no more strangers and foreigners, but

Fellow citizens with the saints, and of the household of God;

20 And are built upon the foundation of the apostles and prophets,

Jesus

IDENTITY IN CHRIST

Christ himself being the chief corner stone;

While we might have different callings, the mandate is still the same winning souls—reaching the souls of men with the gospel of Christ. This is the same commission of the Apostle. Paul preached to the Gentiles. Peter preached to the house of Israel. This gospel must reach to the end of the world until Jesus Christ returns.

Mathews24:14 And this gospel of the kingdom shall be preached in all the world for a

witness unto all nations; and then shall the end come.

The scripture you're referring to, found in Matthew 24:14, encapsulates the essence of the greatest commission bestowed upon us as the followers of Jesus Christ. It's a command that echoes throughout generations, signaling us to spread the gospel of the kingdom to every corner of the earth. In these words, there's a profound calling, a divine assignment entrusted to those who choose to walk in the footsteps of Christ.

Embedded within this scripture is the urgency and universality of the mission. The mandate is clear: the message of salvation isn't confined by borders or boundaries but is meant to cross the globe, reaching every nation, tribe, and tongue.

It's a proclamation that transcends cultural divides, socioeconomic inequalities, and linguistic barriers. The gospel is for all, and its dissemination is pivotal in paving the way for the culmination of time.

As a follower of Jesus Christ, you're not merely a passive spectator but an active participant in the souls of men and women. You're called to be a herald of hope, a vessel through which the light of truth shines into the darkness of the world.

Your assignment isn't relegated to the confines of a church building or a specific locale but extends to the ends of the earth. It's a commission that demands your dedication, your passion, and your unwavering commitment.

In embracing your role within the great commission, you're invited into a partnership with the divine. You become a co-laborer with God, joining hands with fellow believers across continents and cultures. Together, you form a global tapestry of faith, each thread contributing to the vibrant display of God's love and redemption.

Yet, the task before you is not without its challenges. You'll encounter opposition, resistance, and obstacles along the way. There will be moments of doubt, of uncertainty when the enormity of the mission seems overwhelming. But in those moments, you're reminded of the promise embedded within the scripture: that the gospel will be preached in all the world as a witness to all nations.

This promise serves as both an assurance and a catalyst for action. It's a reminder that despite the odds, and the adversity, the mission will ultimately prevail. And as you press forward in faith, you become a living testament to the transformative power of the gospel.

Your journey as a disciple of Christ is intricately woven into the fabric of God's redemptive plan. Every encounter and conversation becomes an opportunity to fulfill the commission entrusted to you. Whether through words spoken or deeds, you have the privilege of being a channel of God's grace, extending His invitation of reconciliation to a broken and hurting world.

So, as you contemplate the magnitude of the task before you, take heart in the words of Matthew 24:14. Let it serve as a rallying cry, igniting within you a fervent zeal to see the gospel proclaimed to the ends of the earth. For in fulfilling this commission, you not only participate in the ushering in of the end times but also in the ushering in of God's kingdom here on earth.

In studying the life of John the Baptist, we find that in his calling, the assignment, the office, and the name were embedded before birth. The was no confusion about what was his destiny. Contrary, we have believers who crossover offices or gifts, not knowing where they belong. Zechariah tarried in the spirit of patience until He received what was promised to him. And this promise what John, who was to walk in the spirit and power of Elijah—walking in fellowship with the Most High God.

As he was from the tribe Levi, he walked in the highest calling of priesthood. Thus, John performed the act of righteousness when he baptized Jesus Christ. Even though he felt unworthy to baptize Christ. It was the commission of the Lord. And I have to say this, John was walking in the priesthood of Melchizedek—the highest order of priesthood. He was not ordained in Jerusalem, or from the house of Levi. He was the prophet of the Most High, in other words, ordained by the Most High just like Moses, Elijah, and Samuel.

John the Baptist's ordination as a prophet is attributed to God Himself. According to the biblical scriptures, John's birth was foretold by an angel to his father, Zechariah, who was serving as a priest in the temple. The angel, Gabriel, announced to Zechariah that his wife, Elizabeth, would bear a son who would be named John and would be filled with the Holy Spirit even from his mother's womb (Luke 1:13-17).

John's role as a prophet was divinely ordained from before his birth. He was chosen by God to prepare the way for the coming of the Messiah, Jesus Christ. John's ministry of baptizing repentant sinners and preaching about the kingdom of God was a fulfillment of Old Testament prophecies, particularly Isaiah 40:3, which describes a voice crying out in the wilderness, preparing the way for the Lord.

Throughout the Gospels, it's clear that John's authority and calling as a prophet were recognized by the people of his time. He was seen as a significant figure, with crowds flocking to hear his message and to receive baptism from him. Even Jesus Himself testified to John's prophetic role, referring to him as more than a prophet (Matthew 11:9) and affirming the importance of his ministry in fulfilling God's purposes.

In essence, John the Baptist's ordination as a prophet stemmed from God's sovereign choice and divine plan. He was set apart from birth to fulfill a crucial role in preparing the way for the coming of Jesus Christ and proclaiming the message of repentance and salvation to the people of Israel.

Countless figures in the bible had the honor to be named by God. The name itself is imbedded with purpose and destiny. In the old times, there were three offices; the office of the Prophets, the Priesthood, and the office of the king. Prophet Samuel operated in both; the prophet and priest. He also judged but in all of these offices, you have the authority to act as judge.

We find David operating in all of these offices. Jesus Christ also, He is the highest priest of our new covenant. He reigns in the heavenly as the king of kings. While on earth, He called himself a prophet.

When you step into the call of God as a man of God, first and foremost, the power has to be in your name. we receive new names when we are in Christ. You are no longer an ordinary person but a child of God. We are translated from being servants to the sons of the Most High. Apart from general identity in the Lord, you receive a personal revelation from the Lord about who you are, what lineage, and what line of prophetic or priestly club you are from.

. . . .

THE PROPHETIC OFFICES never expire. John had to walk in the spirit and power of Elijah who lived thousands of years ago. Even to this day, the office of John is still very much alive—the message of the man of God, John the Baptist, is still very much alive and the core foundation of our Christian beliefs.

This is the message of repentance. John preached repentance. Christ preached repentance. Apostle Peter and Paul also herald the message of salvation, of which repentance is the key. This is what we need in the body of Christ. I know that many get angry or puffed up when you speak about repentance. However, this is the message of salvation, the message of transformation. Repentance is love. When we love God, we follow the commandments. Love is the greatest commandment. Likewise, when you love Christ, you honor his teachings.

John 8:31-32 Then said Jesus to those Jews which believed on him, If ye continue in

my word, then are ye my disciples indeed;

32 And ye shall know the truth, and the truth shall make you free.

John 8:51 Verily, verily, I say unto you, If a man keep my saying, he shall never

see death.

Keeping the Word of God is the highest call of ever believer. If we are not keeping his words, we are deceiving ourselves. As I am talking about the assignment of God, hearing the voice of God and being obedience to the voice should be your number one goal. We should not only glamorous our calling while leaving the source of the call in the background. Intimacy with God is paramount. Those who abide under the shadow of the Most High God shall never run out of strength.

Psalm 68:34 Ascribe ye strength unto God: his excellency is over Israel, and his
strength is in the clouds.

Seeing yourself in light of Scriptures.

Isaiah 40:3-5 The voice of him that crieth in the wilderness, Prepare ye the way of the
LORD, make straight in the desert a highway for our God.
4 Every valley shall be exalted, and every mountain and hill shall be made
low: and the crooked shall be made straight, and the rough places plain:
5 And the glory of the LORD shall be revealed, and all flesh shall see it
together: for the mouth of the LORD hath spoken it.

It is so fascinating that John the Baptist was prophesied before-hand. This is the prophecy of Prophet Isaiah foreseeing the man of the wilderness crying for righteousness and holiness. And the Pharisee came and asked him "Who art thou" and he responded "I am *The voice of him that crieth in the wilderness, Prepare ye the way of the LORD, make straight in the desert a highway for our God.*

When a man has found himself in the pages of the scripture, he has found his own identity. He has found his purpose.

Let us look deeper into this scripture pertaining to John's identity and assignment.

Interpreting Isaiah 40:3-5 in the light of John the Baptist and the concept of identity in Christ carries profound significance.

1. **John the Baptist as a Model**: John the Baptist is often seen as the fulfillment of Isaiah's prophecy, as he prepared the way for Jesus Christ. His role was to prepare hearts for the coming of the Lord, echoing the cry in the wilderness

to "Prepare ye the way of the LORD." Similarly, in our lives, embracing the Scriptures allows us to align ourselves with God's purposes, preparing our hearts for His work. John's humility and dedication to his mission serve as an example for us to align our lives with the will of God as revealed in Scripture.

2. **Understanding Identity in Christ**: The imagery of valleys being exalted, mountains and hills made low, and crooked paths straightened speaks to the transformative power of encountering Christ. When we encounter Jesus and embrace His teachings as revealed in Scripture, our lives undergo a profound change. Our priorities shift, our values realign, and our perspective on ourselves and the world around us is transformed. Just as the landscape is altered to make way for the Lord, so too are our hearts and minds reshaped to reflect His glory.

3. **Revelation of the Glory of the LORD**: The ultimate goal of aligning ourselves with the Scriptures and embracing our identity in Christ is to reveal the glory of the Lord. When we live by God's Word, His glory shines through us, illuminating the world around us. This transformation isn't just personal; it impacts all those around us. Isaiah prophesies that "all flesh shall see it together," highlighting the universal impact of living in alignment with God's truth.

In an instant, aligning ourselves with Scripture, akin to the role of John the Baptist, and embracing our identity in Christ leads to a transformation that prepares the way for the Lord in our lives and reveals His glory to the world. It's a journey of humility, obedience, and alignment with God's will, ultimately leading to a profound impact on ourselves and those around us.

We also have to look at Christ as he is the example of our faith.

Let's embark on a journey of discovery and revelation together, diving into the beautiful truth found in Scripture. In Luke 4:12, we witness a pivotal moment where Jesus, our Savior, unrolls the scroll in the synagogue and reads from the book of Isaiah. In doing so, He unveils His mission, and His purpose here on earth, as described in Isaiah 61:1.

Picture this scene with me: Jesus, surrounded by eager listeners, takes His place in the synagogue. The anticipation is palpable as He unfurls the ancient scroll, His eyes scanning the words penned by the prophet Isaiah. Then, with clarity and conviction, He begins to read:

"The Spirit of the Lord is upon me, because he has anointed me to proclaim good news to the poor. He has sent me to proclaim liberty to the captives and recovering of sight to the blind, to set at liberty those who are oppressed, to proclaim the year of the Lord's favor." (Luke 4:18-19)

In these words, we find the heartbeat of Jesus' mission. He came to bring good news, to release the captives from their chains, to restore sight to the blind, and to lift the burdens of the oppressed. This mission wasn't just a calling for Him; it was His very identity. And as believers, it becomes our identity too, woven into the fabric of our being by the grace of God.

You see, dear one when Jesus declared these words, He wasn't just speaking about Himself; He was speaking about us—about you and me. For in Christ, we find our truest selves. In Him, we discover our purpose, our calling, and our mission here on earth. Just as Jesus was anointed by the Spirit to carry out His mission, so too are we anointed as His followers, empowered to continue the work He began.

So, how do we see ourselves in light of Jesus' mission? We see ourselves as carriers of hope, bearers of love, and vessels of His grace. We see ourselves as agents of transformation, bringing light into the darkest corners of this world. We see ourselves as co-laborers with Christ, partnering with Him to bring about His kingdom here on earth.

But perhaps even more importantly, we see ourselves as beloved children of God, cherished and adored beyond measure. We see ourselves through the lens of His unfailing love, knowing that our worth and identity are found not in what we do, but in who we are.

So, dear believer, take heart and be encouraged. You are not alone on this journey. God has called you, chosen you, and equipped you to fulfill His mission here on earth. And as you walk in the footsteps of Jesus, may you experience the joy of seeing His kingdom come and His will be done, on earth as it is in heaven. Amen.

5 ways of Seeing Yourself in the Scriptures

1. **Daily Scripture Meditation**: Set aside time each day to read and meditate on God's Word. As you immerse yourself in scripture, ask the Holy Spirit to reveal truths about who you are in Christ. Look for passages that speak to your identity as a beloved child of God, redeemed and chosen by Him. Allow these truths to sink deep into your heart and mind, reshaping your perspective and reinforcing your identity in Christ.

2. **Confession and Affirmation**: Speak God's Word over your life daily. Create personalized affirmations based on scripture that declare who you are in Christ. For example, you might say, "I am fearfully and wonderfully made" (Psalm 139:14) or "I am more than a conqueror through Him who loves me" (Romans 8:37). By confessing these truths regularly, you reinforce your identity in Christ and combat negative thoughts and doubts.

3. **Community and Accountability**: Surround yourself with fellow believers who can encourage and support you on your journey of faith. Share your struggles and victories, and hold each other accountable to living out your identity in Christ. Participate in small groups, Bible studies, or church communities where you can grow together in your understanding of scripture and your identity as followers of Jesus.

4. **Service and Ministry**: Engage in acts of service and ministry that align with your identity in Christ. Look

for opportunities to love and serve others as Jesus did, whether through volunteering, outreach programs, or acts of kindness in your daily life. By actively living out your faith and serving others in Jesus' name, you reinforce your identity as a disciple of Christ and reflect His love to the world.

5. **Prayer and Surrender**: Spend time in prayer, inviting God to transform your heart and mind according to His Word. Surrender your fears, insecurities, and doubts to Him, and ask Him to replace them with the truth of who you are in Christ. Allow the Holy Spirit to work in you, molding you into the image of Jesus and empowering you to live out your identity as a child of God.

By implementing these practical steps into your daily life, you can deepen your understanding of scripture and strengthen your identity in Christ. Remember that your identity is rooted in Him, and as you draw closer to Him through His Word and prayer, you will increasingly reflect His love, grace, and truth to the world around you.

Who you identify you, influences you.

As the children of God, we must identify ourselves with our Father who has given us Christ as an example to modify our faith. Christ is the perfect example of our faith, and our faith cannot fail as it is He who strengthens us. It is the teaching of Christ that gives life. His words are spirit and life.

The words of Jesus Christ are "spirit and life" in John 6:63. This statement holds profound significance because it encapsulates the transformative power and divine authority inherent in His teachings. His teachings are transformative, powerful and life giving. The kingdom of Christ is the kingdom of demonstration of the power of words. Thus, you should be caution of what comes out of your mouth. The scriptures say "Life and death are in the power of the tongue".

When you identity yourself with Christ, He influences you. Your thoughts are transformed in light with scriptures. Whatsoever that is above, that is pure, holy, and that is love, you start thinking in line of those because you are covered by the light of the spirit of God. Identity in Christ is victory. Christ always win. You will no longer be obsessed with what people think about you, and their opinion will not matter that much as you identify with the God of the universe who think good thoughts and promising future for you.

Allow the words of Christ to comfort your heart and mend your soul. Any other words that ever hurt you, does not matter. What matters is what Christ think of you. Christ sees you as the winner, and as a powerful being capable of achieving more. You can do all things through Christ who strengthens you.

There are so many things that can weaken our subconscious mind. With all these technologies we praise, we should be cautious with it. Your eyes and your ears are portal in spirit. whatsoever that you receive that is not from the Lord, weakens your spirit. you grow when you feed your soul with the soulful food—the Word of God.

Influences many not only comes from your family and friend circle. It can also come from the society and culture we live in. We live in the culture dominated by media and technology. We should never allow technology to give us identity of who we should be. Our identity is in Christ who has triumphed over the princes of this world. This world is ruled by mighty spirits of darkness that if you are not in Christ, you will be the victim of destruction.

Ephesians 1:20 Which he wrought in Christ, when he raised him from the dead, and set
him at his own right hand in the heavenly places,
21 Far above all principality, and power, and might, and dominion, and
every name that is named, not only in this world, but also in that which is to
come:

Christ is far above the wisdom of this world. He is far above media and technology that rules our everyday life. There are some people who cannot live without, Instagram, Facebook or Twitter. These things dictate many lives that these are the first thing many look up to everyday when they wake up instead of a little prayer of thanksgiving. We do not have problem with technology, however, it stands a chance to be an idol of this age. And it has a level of influence over many lives that we try to live up to the standard of social media.

IDENTITY IN CHRIST

Identity issue is the greatest problem so far. When you are not sure of who you are, you stand at the edge of defeat because somebody else will give it to you. Let God be the truth and all men be liars. Let the word of truth direct your soul, spirit and body. Enter into the secret place with the God of the universe, you will never be the same. The light of God is what change man from seeing things from a man's perspective but from the God's perspective.

The difference from the men of the time of Jesus and Jesus Christ, was that Christ saw things from a heavenly perspective. While they saw things from carnality or from a religious view.

The mind of Christ is the will of God. Every believer ought to have the mind of Christ. The selfless mind that advances the kingdom of God and humanity in general through the mercy, grace and love of God. Adam died when he disconnected from God. Not a physical death but a spiritual death whereby your mind, will, and emotions are disconnected from the spirit of God. It means that when you listen to other voices that are not from God, you stand a high chance to be deceived. The law of God should be in your mouth daily. This is the highest meditation. A man cannot live by bread alone but by every word that comes out of the mouth of God. The word of the king is power.

The mouth of God created all these amazing things we see on this planet. Christ also showed us the demonstration of the power of the Word of God. This Word is the essence of our being. We are because of the Word of power from the Most High. As we come from the Most High, as we are the children of the Most High, we are the children of the Word, we live and breathe the same breath of God, which is the sound of victory.

1 John 5: 4 For whatsoever is born of God overcometh the world: and this is the victory that overcometh the world, even our faith.

Born of God means born of spirit. God is spirit, and all that worship Him must worship Him in spirit and truth. Born of God means you walk in the way, truth and life of Christ. Christ revealed the heart of the Father more than any prophet that ever lived. Thus if you want to know God, Christ is the way.

A practical way is to meditate on the teaching of the Apostles and obey the commandments of love. Love is the theme of center of Christianity. Love, faith and hope. Relationship with the world is an enmity to God, relationship with Christ worth more than this world. Keep your heart in the love of God and your mind transformed by the mighty spirit of God.

I can safely say that all human beings will wrestle with their identity at some point in their lifetime. While I was contemplating writing this book, I did not have set of chapter to include. But that changed along the way as I received word of knowledge from the Holy Spirit about some of the things that majority go through as far as identity crisis go. I had these words in my spirit "The role of mothers and fathers". I knew at that point the responsibility parents has in molding the identity of children.

The Lord hold parents and family accountable for the identity of their children. He chose Abraham because he knew that Abraham will command the generation after him about the ways of the Lord. The best investment parents can do is to teach kids about the ways of the Lord. Individuals are built by community. Community has a big influence in the upbringing of its citizens. The community of believers can do much more by creating a healthy environment of love, hope and faith in the lives of youth.

The enemy does not want you to know who you are. He wants you be unstable in your persona and walk in defeat. It is an opportunity of the enemy to bring you down if ever he observes that you have identity crisis. If you come from a family where you have been told "You are worthless" "You will never amount to nothing" "You are ugly" and more similar sentiments like these, you are bound to have identity crisis. Usually depression and feeling of rejection stems from these.

Words are powerful and can never be erased. It is vital for us to choose our words wisely. Speak whatsoever that you believe will exhort and comfort community. Many of us are hurt because of the broken family we come from. But in God we are accepted, chosen, loved and best of all, eternally forgiven and loved unconditionally.

Proverb 16:13 Righteous lips are the delight of kings; and they love him that speaketh

right.

Truth saves. Truth set us free. Righteous lips are delightful to people. In family and in the community, the lips that spill righteous are as honeycomb and sweet to the soul. Growing up in the family that has the lips of the knowledge of God is healthy environment for children. Teach the young of the ways of the Lord and when they grow up, they will never forget their roots.

Proverb 16:24 Pleasant words are as an honeycomb, sweet to the soul, and health to the bones.

Identity in Christ.
Chosen before Creation.

1. *Ephesians 1:4-5 (NIV) - "For he chose us in him before the creation of the world to be holy and blameless in his sight. In love, he predestined us for adoption to sonship through Jesus Christ."*

God values us more than any other species or creature in this planet. He had us in His mind even before He created us. There is no mistake in the creation of God. We sometimes feel worthless at some point in life, however, we shouldn't allow circumstance to determine or undermine our value. We are valuable than diamonds and rubies.

While in this world we maybe be obsessed with flashy things like diamond and gold, in the kingdom of God we will walk on it. Like Jeremiah, God knew us before He birthed us. Our calling and assignment are wrapped our spirit being. God created spirit being before manifestation. We were created to have deep intimacy with God just like Adam in the garden of Eden before the fall.

Adam's mind was connected to God. When God thought, Adam knew the thoughts, the mind and the will of God. He had all the gifts of the spirit and all the spiritual discernment. But that was before the enemy infiltrated their mind through Eve.

We were also created to be a holy nation. Adam was a prophet, priest and king. He had a special way of communicating with God. He knew the mind and the will of God that he was to teach his children after him in the ways of the Lord. God was talking to Adam all this time, not Eve. Adam was to be a priest of his family and teach the ways of the Lord. This is the mystery of marriage. It is a spiritual union with God before husband and wife.

The man represents God, and he is also the priest of his family. The wife assists husband in his godly duty. The wife honors and respect the destiny God has bestowed upon the man. A holy nation starts in the family, in marriage before the community. Abraham taught his family in the ways of the Lord. His family was an extension of the image of Christ. This is what God need. A holy nation under the umbrella of the love of God that takes the gospel of Christ to the end of the world. Love always wins. Where there is love, there is no defeat. In love he has predestined us for adoption of sonship through Jesus Christ.

Sons and daughters of Christ are born of spirit. They are the overcomers because they are born of God. Son inherit what the Father has, and does what the Father does. Son is an extension of the image of the Father. The image of the Father is the spirit of truth. The image of the Father is the light of glory. The image of the Father is wisdom, knowledge and understanding. The image of the Father is the demonstration of the power of the Word.

John 1:3 In the beginning was the Word, and the Word was with
God, and the
Word was God.
2 The same was in the beginning with God.
3 All things were made by him; and without him was not any thing
made
that was made.

The image of God is the Word. Christ is the Living Word. A man cannot live by bread alone but by every word that comes out of the mouth of God. Live the Word, eat the Word, and speak the Word. Your life would never be the same.

We are the children of God.

1. 1 John 3:1 (NIV) - "See what great love the Father has lavished on us, that we should be called children of God! And that is what we are!"

We are no longer strangers in the kingdom of God. We are no longer alienated from God. The great love of God is upon us. The Father of our Lord Jesus Christ love us through the death of Christ on the cross. Cross has to be the emblem of love, grace and mercy.

It is a big thing to be the child of God. You are born of spirit and hopeful of the eternal salvation of God. Because there is life beyond what our eyes can see. Therefore, in Christ we are assured of ETERNAL GLORY for our soul rest.

What we are—the children of God born in spirit and truth. God is spirit.

John 4:24 God is a Spirit: and they that worship him must worship him in spirit and
in truth.

When the Father loves his son or daughter, He will provide everything the son or the daughter needs. Eventually the Son has to inherit whatsoever the Father has. The blessings and gifts of the household of the Father are for His children. This is so to God through His Son Jesus Christ.

I once had a spiritual vision in the heavenly realm, where I had an encounter with the God of the universe, and He was looking at the face of Christ deeply, after looking at Christ, He looked at me. And I got it in my spirit that when God looks at Christ, He sees us. We are in Christ, and Christ is in God. We are the image of Christ with the power of Sonship. We are co-heir with Christ. Christ came in this world for His brothers and sisters, and we are his own. Never feel alone and left out, Christ is your best friend!

As much as God beholds the face of His Son, we are to behold the face of Christ.

Psalm 34:5 They looked unto him, and were lightened: and their faces were not ashamed.

Look unto Christ the hope of your glory and salvation, you shall not be ashamed. The beauty and the glory of His face is the light of victory. In Him is power, and riches, and wisdom, and strength, and honour, and glory, and blessing. Amen!

We are new Creation.

1. 2 Corinthians 5:17 (NIV) - "Therefore, if anyone is in Christ, the new creation has come: The old has gone, the new is here!"

A new creature is a spirit born believer. Who walks in the power of Sonship. Salvation gives us a second chance of life of God. God resides in our mortal body by His mighty spirit of grace and comfort. The old life of sin, the old life of anti-Christ spirit is gone. And we are grafted in the commonwealth of Israel through the Abrahamic promise.

A new creature is a changed mind, changed perspective, and a changed attitude in the things of God. As Christ was zealous about God's business, thus a new creature has to be all about the kingdom of God. The life of a believer is not a smooth ride, there a valleys and hills, but when you have Christ you have everything! You carry the cross of Jesus Christ. Cross is our emblem of triumph and victory.

In God you are a new person. You no longer self-dependent on you own strength and ability but allow the wisdom, the knowledge and understanding of God takes the lead through the Holy Spirit.

Psalm 20:7 Some trust in chariots, and some in horses: but we will remember the
name of the LORD our God.

In all things we remember the name of the Lord. In thanksgiving, worship and praise, we exalt the excellent name of the Lord of glory. Someone who trust all the way in the Lord shall never be ashamed. Total depended in the Lord is the medicine to our soul, spirit and body.

Heirs of God and Co-heirs with Christ.

1. *Romans 8:17 (NIV) - "Now if we are children, then we are heirs—heirs of God and co-heirs with Christ, if indeed we share in his sufferings in order that we may also share in his glory."*

We share in His suffering and also in His glory. We belong in the big family of grace, love and mercy—the family of God which is the house of prayer. God sees Christ in us, we are part of the Godhead. Heirs are the inheritors of the kingdom of God and the treasures of the kingdom of God. Heirs are also the successors, they take from where Christ left and continue the legacy.

Christ rules in the third heaven. It means we also rule with Him as we are the Co-heirs with Him. We are raised up in Christ seated in the heavenly places. From above we come, and from above we are. Folks, see yourself in the heavenly places where Christ dwells far above principalities and dominions.

Ephesians 2:6 And hath raised us up together, and made us sit to-gether in heavenly places in Christ Jesus:

Ephesians 1:20 Which he wrought in Christ, when he raised him from the dead, and set

him at his own right hand in the heavenly places,

21 Far above all principality, and power, and might, and dominion, and

every name that is named, not only in this world, but also in that which is to

come:

From these two scriptures above, it is a testament that we are powerful beings adopted to Sonship through the grace of God and Christ. The enemy is already defeated. Even though he is, he would never stop making noise—making it seem as if the bad guy is winning.

Satan is the god of this world. We cannot deny that. But a god with a small letter. Greater is He that is in us than he that is in the world. Follow God and the teaching of Jesus Christ, you shall never be moved. Intimacy with God is a remedy to make the devil back off in your life.

Men and women with deep prayer lives can shake the pillars of the kingdom of Satan to the ground. The prayer of the righteous amount and abound. Never forget that you are the citizen of heaven where all lights dwell. Never forget that you are the light of the world. Even in dare times, never speak down on yourself but the truth of the scriptures. Your identity is in the spirit of truth—Jesus Christ Himself.

Chosen People, Royal Priesthood, and God's special possession.

1. *1 Peter 2:9 (NIV) - "But you are a chosen people, a royal priesthood, a holy nation, God's special possession, that you may declare the praises of him who called you out of darkness into his wonderful light."*

We did not choose Him but He chose us before the creation of the world. To be chosen is better than to be called. It means you are valuable and special when you are chosen. And that's what God did! He chose you for the greater glory, honor and power. He lifts you up, exalt you, and have you walk in spirit of excellency. Praise Him for His mighty act. By His mighty arm of deliverance, He has called you out of darkness into the wonderful light of glory.

With all what God has done in your life, let the highest praise come out of your mouth and exalt the Lord of glory. There are 5 things that we have to look at in the scripture above:

- You are chosen people.
- A royal priesthood.
- A Holy nation.
- God's special possession.
- Called out of darkness into light.

A Royal Priesthood:

In Christ, you are part of a royal priesthood, a chosen and honored group set apart for God's divine purposes. This identity carries with it a profound sense of dignity and responsibility. Just as ancient priests served as mediators between God and humanity, you have been called to represent God's love and grace to the world.

As a member of this royal priesthood, you have direct access to God's presence. You can approach Him with confidence, knowing that you are His beloved child and a co-heir with Christ. Your prayers and worship are pleasing to Him, and your life is a living sacrifice, holy and acceptable in His sight.

Embrace your identity as a royal priest with humility and reverence. Allow God to use you as His instrument of blessing and reconciliation in the world. Let your words and actions reflect the love and compassion of Christ, drawing others into His kingdom and His eternal priesthood.

A Holy Nation:

In Christ, you are part of a holy nation, a community of believers set apart for God's glory. This identity speaks to your belonging and your citizenship in the kingdom of God. You are no longer defined by earthly boundaries or divisions but by your unity in Christ with fellow believers from every tribe, tongue, and nation.

As a member of this holy nation, you are called to live a life of holiness and righteousness. You are set apart for God's purposes, called to be a light in the darkness and a beacon of hope to the lost and broken. Your actions and attitudes should reflect the character of Christ, drawing others into the kingdom and reflecting God's glory to the world.

Embrace your identity as a citizen of the holy nation with gratitude and humility. Let your life be a reflection of the transformative power of God's grace, shining brightly in a world that desperately needs His light. And may you always remember that you are part of a chosen people, a holy nation, beloved by God and called to live for His glory.

God's Special Possession:

In Christ, you are God's special possession, treasured and cherished beyond measure. This identity speaks to your worth and value in the eyes of your Heavenly Father. You are not just a random collection of atoms or a face in the crowd, but a precious jewel in His crown, crafted with love and care.

As God's special possession, you are deeply loved and cared for. Your Heavenly Father knows you intimately, and He delights in every aspect of your being. He rejoices over you with singing, and He has plans for your life that are good and full of hope.

Embrace your identity as God's special possession with confidence and assurance. Let go of any doubts or insecurities about your worth, and instead, rest in the knowledge that you are deeply loved and valued by the One who created the heavens and the earth. And may you always live in the light of His love, knowing that you are His and He is yours, now and forevermore.

Called Out of Darkness into Light:

In Christ, you have been called out of darkness into His marvelous light. This identity speaks to your journey from spiritual blindness and ignorance to the knowledge and truth found in Jesus Christ. You are no longer enslaved to sin and death but have been set free by the power of His resurrection.

As one who has been called out of darkness into light, you are called to live as a child of light. Your life is a testimony to the transformative power of God's grace, shining brightly in a world that desperately needs His truth and love. You are called to walk in righteousness and holiness, reflecting the glory of God to those around you.

Embrace your identity as one who has been called out of darkness into light with joy and gratitude. Let your life be a beacon of hope to the lost and broken, pointing them to the One who can bring them out of darkness into His marvelous light. And may you always walk in the light of His presence, knowing that you are loved, forgiven, and redeemed by the One who called you out of darkness into His marvelous light.

I am sanctified and Justified.

1. *1 Corinthians 6:11 (NIV) - "And that is what some of you were. But you were washed, you were sanctified, you were justified in the name of the Lord Jesus Christ and by the Spirit of our God."*

In the eyes of Christ, you are sanctified and justified. These words carry immense power and meaning, shaping your identity in a profound way. Let's delve into what this means for you.

To be sanctified means to be set apart, made holy, and purified. It signifies that you are no longer bound by the chains of sin and darkness. Instead, you are set apart for a divine purpose, chosen by God Himself. Imagine standing in the presence of the Almighty, washed clean of all impurities, shining with the radiance of His grace. That's who you are—a beloved child of God, purified by His unfailing love.

Moreover, you are justified. This means that through Christ, you are declared righteous, acquitted of all guilt and shame. Your past mistakes, your flaws, your shortcomings—none of them define you anymore. In the eyes of God, you are blameless, clothed in the righteousness of Christ. It's as if you've been given a clean slate, a fresh start to embrace the fullness of life that God has intended for you.

Reflect on these truths: you are sanctified, you are justified. Let these words sink deep into your soul, bringing comfort and assurance. You are not defined by your past or your failures. You are defined by the love and grace of Jesus Christ, who gave everything so that you could be made new.

In Christ, you find your true identity—a beloved child of God, cherished beyond measure. You are not alone on this journey. The Spirit of God dwells within you, guiding you, strengthening you, and empowering you to live a life that honors Him.

When doubts assail you and fears threaten to overwhelm, remember who you are in Christ. You are sanctified, set apart for God's glorious purposes. You are justified, declared righteous through the sacrifice of Jesus Christ. Let these truths anchor your soul, filling you with hope and confidence.

Embrace your identity in Christ with gratitude and humility. Walk in the freedom that comes from knowing that you are loved, accepted, and chosen by God. Let His grace transform you from the inside out, shaping you into the person He created you to be.

So, dear friend, rejoice in who you are in Christ. You are sanctified, you are justified—forever cherished, forever loved, forever secure in the embrace of your Heavenly Father.

Nothing can separate me from the Love of God.

1. *Romans 8:38-39 (NIV) - "For I am convinced that neither death nor life, neither angels nor demons, neither the present nor the future, nor any powers, neither height nor depth, nor anything else in all creation, will be able to separate us from the love of God that is in Christ Jesus our Lord."*

In the depths of your soul, hold fast to this truth: nothing can separate you from the love of God. Let these words resonate within you, filling you with a profound sense of security and peace. For in Christ, you are enveloped in a love that surpasses all understanding, a love that knows no bounds.

Consider the magnitude of this love. It transcends every barrier, every obstacle, every force in the universe. Neither death nor life, neither angels nor demons, neither the present nor the future—nothing can stand between you and the boundless love of God. It is a love that defies comprehension, stretching beyond the limits of human understanding.

In moments of doubt or despair, remember this truth: you are eternally held in the embrace of God's love. No matter what trials or tribulations may come your way, His love remains steadfast and unwavering. It is a love that endures through every storm, offering solace in times of sorrow and hope in times of despair.

Ponder the depths of God's love for you. It is a love that knows no conditions, no prerequisites. You do not have to earn it or deserve it—it is freely given, poured out upon you without measure. Even when you falter or stumble, His love remains constant, never wavering or fading away.

Reflect on the magnitude of God's love. It reaches to the highest heights and the deepest depths, encompassing every aspect of your being. There is nowhere you can go, no place you can hide, where His love cannot find you. It is a love that pursues you relentlessly, drawing you ever closer into the warmth of His embrace.

Take comfort in the unshakable truth that nothing—absolutely nothing—can separate you from the love of God. No matter what trials or tribulations may come your way, His love remains your anchor, your rock, your firm foundation. It is a love that transcends time and space, stretching from eternity past to eternity future.

So, dear friend, rest assured in the knowledge that you are forever held in the palm of God's hand. His love surrounds you, sustains you, and empowers you to face whatever challenges may come your way. Nothing can separate you from His love—indeed, it is the greatest gift you will ever know.

Fearfully and wonderfully made.

1. Psalm 139:14 (NIV) - "I praise you because I am fearfully and wonderfully made; your works are wonderful, I know that full well."

You are fearfully and wonderfully made. Let these words sink deep into your heart and soul, for they speak to the incredible beauty and uniqueness of who you are. You are not a mistake or a random occurrence, but a masterpiece crafted by the hands of the Creator Himself.

Reflect on the profound truth that you are fearfully made. This means that God created you with awe and reverence, with careful attention to every detail. You are intricately designed, with a purpose and a plan that only He can fully comprehend. Your existence is not a coincidence, but a deliberate act of divine creation.

Moreover, you are wonderfully made. Consider the wonder and majesty of God's handiwork in your life. From the depths of your soul to the intricacies of your physical form, you are a testament to His greatness. Your unique gifts, talents, and personality traits reflect the infinite creativity of the One who formed you in His image.

Embrace the truth that you are fearfully and wonderfully made. Let go of any doubts or insecurities about yourself, and instead, celebrate the person God has created you to be. You are a reflection of His glory, a living testament to His love and grace.

In moments of self-doubt or struggle, remember these words: you are fearfully and wonderfully made. You are valued, cherished, and deeply loved by the One who knit you together in your mother's womb. Your worth is not determined by external factors or worldly standards, but by the unconditional love of your Heavenly Father.

So, embrace your uniqueness and embrace your identity as a beloved child of God. Walk confidently in the knowledge that you are fearfully and wonderfully made, with a purpose and a destiny that only you can fulfill. Let your life be a testimony to the greatness of the One who created you, and may you always remember the words of the psalmist: "I praise you because I am fearfully and wonderfully made."

Rescued from dominion of darkness.

1. Colossians 1:13-14 (NIV) - "For he has rescued us from the dominion of darkness and brought us into the kingdom of the Son he loves, in whom we have redemption, the forgiveness of sins."

You have been rescued from the dominion of darkness. Let this truth anchor your soul and fill you with gratitude and awe. You were once trapped in the grip of sin and despair, but through the power of Christ, you have been set free.

Reflect on the magnitude of this rescue mission. God, in His infinite love and mercy, reached down into the depths of darkness to rescue you. He saw your brokenness and your need for redemption, and He acted decisively to save you. It was not by your own strength or merit, but by His grace alone that you were lifted out of darkness and brought into the kingdom of light.

Consider the contrast between darkness and light. In darkness, there is fear, confusion, and hopelessness. But in the kingdom of light, there is freedom, clarity, and eternal hope. You have been brought into this kingdom through the sacrifice of Jesus Christ, the Son Whom God loves. His love knows no bounds, and through Him, you have received redemption and the forgiveness of sins.

Embrace your identity as a rescued child of God. You are no longer defined by your past or your mistakes. You have been washed clean by the blood of Christ, clothed in His righteousness, and welcomed into the family of God. You are a new creation, with a new purpose and a new destiny in Him.

In moments of weakness or temptation, remember that you have been rescued from the dominion of darkness. You are no longer under its power or its influence. Instead, you belong to the kingdom of light, where Christ reigns supreme. His power is made perfect in your weakness, and His grace is more than sufficient for all your needs.

So, live boldly and confidently as a rescued child of God. Walk in the freedom and the victory that Christ has won for you. Let your life be a testament to His saving power and His unfailing love. And may you always rejoice in the truth that you have been rescued from the dominion of darkness and brought into the glorious light of His kingdom.

Christ lives in me.

1. *Galatians 2:20 (NIV) - "I have been crucified with Christ and I no longer live, but Christ lives in me. The life I now live in the body, I live by faith in the Son of God, who loved me and gave himself for me."*

Christ lives in you. Let this profound truth sink deep into your spirit and transform the way you see yourself and the world around you. You are not alone, for the very presence of Christ dwells within you, guiding, strengthening, and empowering you each step of the way.

Reflect on the significance of this reality: you have been crucified with Christ. Your old self, with its desires and ambitions, has been put to death, and in its place, Christ now lives within you. This is a radical transformation, a divine exchange where your identity is now found in Him.

Consider the implications of Christ living in you. It means that His love, His power, and His grace are constantly at work within you, shaping you into the person God has called you to be. You no longer need to rely on your own strength or wisdom, for Christ Himself is your source of life and strength.

Embrace the life of faith that flows from Christ living in you. It is a life marked by trust and dependence on Him, a life surrendered to His will and His purposes. Every decision you make, every step you take, is guided by faith in the Son of God, who loved you so much that He gave Himself for you.

In moments of doubt or uncertainty, remember that Christ lives in you. His presence is your constant companion, a beacon of hope in the midst of darkness. You are never alone, for He is with you always, walking beside you and working within you to accomplish His good and perfect will.

So, live boldly and confidently as a vessel of Christ's love and grace. Let His light shine through you, illuminating the world with His truth and His goodness. And may you always rejoice in the reality that Christ lives in you, transforming your life from the inside out and empowering you to live a life that honors and glorifies Him.

In Christ 100 Prayer Points

100 prayer points inspired by the identity we have in Christ:

1. In Christ, I am forgiven of all my sins (Ephesians 1:7).
2. In Christ, I am a new creation (2 Corinthians 5:17).
3. In Christ, I am loved unconditionally (Romans 8:38-39).
4. In Christ, I am free from condemnation (Romans 8:1).
5. In Christ, I am accepted by God (Ephesians 1:6).
6. In Christ, I am empowered by the Holy Spirit (Acts 1:8).
7. In Christ, I am blessed with every spiritual blessing (Ephesians 1:3).
8. In Christ, I am an heir of God and co-heir with Christ (Romans 8:17).
9. In Christ, I am victorious over sin and death (1 Corinthians 15:57).
10. In Christ, I am called to fulfill a divine purpose (Ephesians 2:10).
11. In Christ, I am a temple of the Holy Spirit (1 Corinthians 6:19).
12. In Christ, I am filled with joy and peace (Romans 15:13).
13. In Christ, I am clothed with righteousness (Isaiah 61:10).
14. In Christ, I am made strong in my weakness (2 Corinthians 12:9).
15. In Christ, I am equipped to do good works (Ephesians 2:10).
16. In Christ, I am surrounded by His protection (Psalm 91:11).

17. In Christ, I am led by His guidance (Psalm 32:8).
18. In Christ, I am part of His body, the Church (1 Corinthians 12:27).
19. In Christ, I am called to love others as He loves me (John 13:34).
20. In Christ, I am called to walk in humility and grace (Colossians 3:12).
21. In Christ, I am given wisdom and discernment (James 1:5).
22. In Christ, I am an overcomer through faith (1 John 5:4).
23. In Christ, I am made worthy of His calling (2 Thessalonians 1:11).
24. In Christ, I am a light in this world (Matthew 5:14).
25. In Christ, I am called to bear fruit that lasts (John 15:16).
26. In Christ, I am strengthened by His promises (Philippians 4:13).
27. In Christ, I am secure in His unfailing love (Psalm 103:17).
28. In Christ, I am set free from bondage (Galatians 5:1).
29. In Christ, I am given peace that surpasses understanding (Philippians 4:7).
30. In Christ, I am filled with hope for the future (Jeremiah 29:11).
31. In Christ, I am called to walk in righteousness (1 John 2:29).
32. In Christ, I am called to be a peacemaker (Matthew 5:9).
33. In Christ, I am called to forgive others as I've been forgiven (Colossians 3:13).
34. In Christ, I am made alive in Him (Ephesians 2:5).
35. In Christ, I am called to be holy as He is holy (1 Peter

1:16).

36. In Christ, I am a disciple, learning from His teachings (Matthew 28:19).

37. In Christ, I am given the authority to trample on serpents (Luke 10:19).

38. In Christ, I am called to bear one another's burdens (Galatians 6:2).

39. In Christ, I am called to be a faithful steward of His gifts (1 Peter 4:10).

40. In Christ, I am filled with gratitude for His blessings (Colossians 3:17).

41. In Christ, I am called to seek first His kingdom (Matthew 6:33).

42. In Christ, I am called to speak the truth in love (Ephesians 4:15).

43. In Christ, I am called to be patient and kind (1 Corinthians 13:4).

44. In Christ, I am called to be a living sacrifice (Romans 12:1).

45. In Christ, I am called to be faithful in prayer (1 Thessalonians 5:17).

46. In Christ, I am called to persevere in trials (James 1:12).

47. In Christ, I am called to be a servant of all (Mark 10:45).

48. In Christ, I am called to be an ambassador of reconciliation (2 Corinthians 5:20).

49. In Christ, I am called to be generous and cheerful in giving (2 Corinthians 9:7).

50. In Christ, I am called to worship Him in spirit and in truth (John 4:24).

51. In Christ, I am called to abide in His love (John 15:9).

52. In Christ, I am called to be faithful in little things (Luke 16:10).

53. In Christ, I am called to put on the armor of God (Ephesians 6:11).

54. In Christ, I am called to be an example of His love (1 Timothy 4:12).

55. In Christ, I am called to rejoice always (1 Thessalonians 5:16).

56. In Christ, I am called to be content in all circumstances (Philippians 4:11).

57. In Christ, I am called to be a doer of His word (James 1:22).

58. In Christ, I am called to be a witness of His resurrection (Acts 1:8).

59. In Christ, I am called to submit to God and resist the devil (James 4:7).

60. In Christ, I am called to bear the fruit of the Spirit (Galatians 5:22-23).

61. In Christ, I am called to lay aside every weight and sin (Hebrews 12:1).

62. In Christ, I am called to love my enemies and pray for them (Matthew 5:44).

63. In Christ, I am called to be faithful unto death (Revelation 2:10).

64. In Christ, I am called to seek wisdom from above (James 3:17).

65. In Christ, I am called to trust in His provision (Philippians 4:19).

66. In Christ, I am called to be holy in all my conduct (1 Peter 1:15).

67. In Christ, I am called to walk in the light as He is in the light (1 John 1:7).
68. In Christ, I am called to serve others with humility (Philippians 2:3-4).
69. In Christ, I am called to confess my sins and receive His forgiveness (1 John 1:9).
70. In Christ, I am called to be patient in tribulation (Romans 12:12).
71. In Christ, I am called to pursue peace with all people (Hebrews 12:14).
72. In Christ, I am called to be diligent in my work (Proverbs 12:24).
73. In Christ, I am called to honor God with my body (1 Corinthians 6:20).
74. In Christ, I am called to love God with all my heart, soul, and mind (Matthew 22:37).
75. In Christ, I am called to love my neighbor as myself (Matthew 22:39).
76. In Christ, I am called to be sober-minded and alert (1 Peter 5:8).
77. In Christ, I am called to bear one another's burdens (Galatians 6:2).
78. In Christ, I am called to walk by faith, not by sight (2 Corinthians 5:7).
79. In Christ, I am called to be salt and light in the world (Matthew 5:13-16).
80. In Christ, I am called to trust in the Lord with all my heart (Proverbs 3:5-6).
81. In Christ, I am called to seek His kingdom above all else (Matthew 6:33).

82. In Christ, I am called to do justice, love mercy, and walk humbly with God (Micah 6:8).

83. In Christ, I am called to be strong and courageous (Joshua 1:9).

84. In Christ, I am called to be quick to listen, slow to speak, and slow to become angry (James 1:19).

85. In Christ, I am called to forgive others as Christ forgave me (Ephesians 4:32).

86. In Christ, I am called to be a vessel of honor, sanctified and useful to the Master (2 Timothy 2:21).

87. In Christ, I am called to put on the full armor of God, so that I can stand firm against the schemes of the devil (Ephesians 6:11).

88. In Christ, I am called to let the peace of Christ rule in my heart, and to be thankful (Colossians 3:15).

89. In Christ, I am called to set my mind on things above, not on earthly things (Colossians 3:2).

90. In Christ, I am called to walk in love, just as Christ also loved me and gave Himself up for me (Ephesians 5:2).

91. In Christ, I am called to be anxious for nothing, but in everything by prayer and supplication with thanksgiving let my requests be made known to God (Philippians 4:6).

92. In Christ, I am called to let the word of Christ richly dwell within me, with all wisdom teaching and admonishing one another with psalms and hymns and spiritual songs, singing with thankfulness in my heart to God (Colossians 3:16).

93. In Christ, I am called to consider it all joy when I encounter various trials, knowing that the testing of my faith produces endurance (James 1:2-3).

94. In Christ, I am called to be steadfast, immovable, always abounding in the work of the Lord, knowing that my toil is not in vain in the Lord (1 Corinthians 15:58).

95. In Christ, I am called to be filled with the knowledge of His will in all spiritual wisdom and understanding, so that I will walk in a manner worthy of the Lord, to please Him in all respects, bearing fruit in every good work and increasing in the knowledge of God (Colossians 1:9-10).

96. In Christ, I am called to pursue righteousness, godliness, faith, love, perseverance, and gentleness (1 Timothy 6:11).

97. In Christ, I am called to let all bitterness and wrath and anger and clamor and slander be put away from me, along with all malice. I am to be kind to others, tender-hearted, forgiving each other, just as God in Christ also has forgiven me (Ephesians 4:31-32).

98. In Christ, I am called to rejoice always, pray without ceasing, in everything give thanks; for this is God's will for me in Christ Jesus (1 Thessalonians 5:16-18).

99. In Christ, I am called to be strong in the Lord and in the strength of His might. I am to put on the full armor of God, so that I will be able to stand firm against the schemes of the devil (Ephesians 6:10-11).

100. In Christ, I am called to abound in hope by the power of the Holy Spirit (Romans 15:13).

May these prayers bring encouragement, strength, and a deeper understanding of our identity in Christ.

100 prayer points inspired by Psalms, reflecting on the identity we have in Christ:

1. In Christ, I am like a tree planted by streams of water, yielding fruit in due season (Psalm 1:3).
2. In Christ, I find refuge and strength, a very present help in trouble (Psalm 46:1).
3. In Christ, I am blessed, for my sins are forgiven, and my transgressions are covered (Psalm 32:1).
4. In Christ, I rejoice and sing praises to His name, for He has dealt bountifully with me (Psalm 13:6).
5. In Christ, I take delight in His law, meditating on it day and night (Psalm 1:2).
6. In Christ, I lift up my eyes to the hills, knowing my help comes from the Lord, the Maker of heaven and earth (Psalm 121:1-2).
7. In Christ, I am filled with joy and gladness, for His love endures forever (Psalm 30:5).
8. In Christ, I seek His face continually, longing to dwell in His presence forever (Psalm 27:4).
9. In Christ, I call upon His name, knowing He hears me and delivers me from all my fears (Psalm 34:4).
10. In Christ, I trust in His unfailing love, rejoicing in His salvation (Psalm 13:5).
11. In Christ, I find rest for my soul, knowing He is my shepherd, and I lack nothing (Psalm 23:1).
12. In Christ, I praise Him with all my heart, declaring His marvelous deeds among the nations (Psalm 9:1).

13. In Christ, I take refuge under the shadow of His wings, finding my shelter and protection in Him (Psalm 91:4).

14. In Christ, I walk in integrity, for He upholds me and keeps me secure (Psalm 41:12).

15. In Christ, I am filled with hope, waiting patiently for Him, my help and my shield (Psalm 33:20).

16. In Christ, I rejoice in His salvation, singing praises to Him, my strength and my song (Psalm 118:14).

17. In Christ, I seek His face earnestly, thirsting for Him like a deer pants for streams of water (Psalm 42:1).

18. In Christ, I bless the Lord at all times, His praise continually on my lips (Psalm 34:1).

19. In Christ, I find satisfaction in Him alone, delighting in His abundance (Psalm 63:5).

20. In Christ, I am surrounded by His righteousness, His faithfulness reaching to the skies (Psalm 36:5).

21. In Christ, I offer Him the sacrifice of thanksgiving, honoring Him with my praise (Psalm 116:17).

22. In Christ, I rejoice in His presence, singing praises to Him, my rock and my salvation (Psalm 95:1).

23. In Christ, I trust in His mercy, knowing He is my refuge and my fortress (Psalm 91:2).

24. In Christ, I cry out to Him in my distress, and He hears me, delivering me from all my troubles (Psalm 34:6).

25. In Christ, I take refuge in the shadow of His wings, finding my strength and security in Him (Psalm 36:7).

26. In Christ, I praise Him with a joyful heart, singing songs of thanksgiving to Him (Psalm 147:7).

27. In Christ, I rejoice in His salvation, giving thanks to Him and proclaiming His greatness among the nations (Psalm

96:2).

28. In Christ, I seek His face continually, trusting in His steadfast love and faithfulness (Psalm 25:5).

29. In Christ, I lift up my soul to Him, seeking His guidance and direction in all things (Psalm 25:1).

30. In Christ, I give thanks to the Lord, for He is good, and His love endures forever (Psalm 107:1).

31. In Christ, I praise Him with all my heart, declaring His wonders and His glory (Psalm 9:1).

32. In Christ, I sing praises to His name, exalting Him above all gods (Psalm 95:2).

33. In Christ, I trust in His unfailing love, knowing He is my rock and my salvation (Psalm 62:7).

34. In Christ, I rejoice in His presence, finding strength and joy in His Holy Spirit (Psalm 16:11).

35. In Christ, I take refuge in Him, knowing He is my shield and my fortress (Psalm 18:2).

36. In Christ, I seek His face earnestly, longing to dwell in His presence forever (Psalm 27:8).

37. In Christ, I rejoice in His salvation, singing praises to Him, my strength and my song (Psalm 118:21).

38. In Christ, I trust in His unfailing love, knowing He is my refuge and my strength (Psalm 59:16).

39. In Christ, I praise Him with a grateful heart, giving thanks to Him for His goodness and mercy (Psalm 100:4).

40. In Christ, I rejoice in His presence, finding peace and joy in His Holy Spirit (Psalm 16:9).

41. In Christ, I trust in His unfailing love, knowing He is my rock and my salvation (Psalm 62:2).

42. In Christ, I take refuge in Him, finding strength and

security in His mighty hand (Psalm 46:1).

43. In Christ, I seek His face continually, longing to dwell in His presence forever (Psalm 27:4).

44. In Christ, I rejoice in His salvation, singing praises to Him, my strength and my song (Psalm 118:14).

45. In Christ, I trust in His unfailing love, knowing He is my refuge and my fortress (Psalm 91:2).

46. In Christ, I lift up my soul to Him, seeking His guidance and direction in all things (Psalm 25:1).

47. In Christ, I give thanks to the Lord, for He is good, and His love endures forever (Psalm 107:1).

48. In Christ, I praise Him with all my heart, declaring His wonders and His glory (Psalm 9:1).

49. In Christ, I sing praises to His name, exalting Him above all gods (Psalm 95:2).

50. In Christ, I trust in His unfailing love, knowing He is my rock and my salvation (Psalm 62:7).

51. In Christ, I rejoice in His presence, finding strength and joy in His Holy Spirit (Psalm 16:11).

52. In Christ, I take refuge in Him, knowing He is my shield and my fortress (Psalm 18:2).

53. In Christ, I seek His face earnestly, longing to dwell in His presence forever (Psalm 27:8).

54. In Christ, I rejoice in His salvation, singing praises to Him, my strength and my song (Psalm 118:21).

55. In Christ, I trust in His unfailing love, knowing He is my refuge and my strength (Psalm 59:16).

56. In Christ, I praise Him with a grateful heart, giving thanks to Him for His goodness and mercy (Psalm 100:4).

57. In Christ, I rejoice in His presence, finding peace and joy

in His Holy Spirit (Psalm 16:9).

58. In Christ, I trust in His unfailing love, knowing He is my rock and my salvation (Psalm 62:2).

59. In Christ, I take refuge in Him, finding strength and security in His mighty hand (Psalm 46:1).

60. In Christ, I seek His face continually, longing to dwell in His presence forever (Psalm 27:4).

61. In Christ, I rejoice in His salvation, singing praises to Him, my strength and my song (Psalm 118:14).

62. In Christ, I trust in His unfailing love, knowing He is my refuge and my fortress (Psalm 91:2).

63. In Christ, I lift up my soul to Him, seeking His guidance and direction in all things (Psalm 25:1).

64. In Christ, I give thanks to the Lord, for He is good, and His love endures forever (Psalm 107:1).

65. In Christ, I praise Him with all my heart, declaring His wonders and His glory (Psalm 9:1).

66. In Christ, I sing praises to His name, exalting Him above all gods (Psalm 95:2).

67. In Christ, I trust in His unfailing love, knowing He is my rock and my salvation (Psalm 62:7).

68. In Christ, I rejoice in His presence, finding strength and joy in His Holy Spirit (Psalm 16:11).

69. In Christ, I take refuge in Him, knowing He is my shield and my fortress (Psalm 18:2).

70. In Christ, I seek His face earnestly, longing to dwell in His presence forever (Psalm 27:8).

71. In Christ, I rejoice in His salvation, singing praises to Him, my strength and my song (Psalm 118:21).

72. In Christ, I trust in His unfailing love, knowing He is my

refuge and my strength (Psalm 59:16).

73. In Christ, I praise Him with a grateful heart, giving thanks to Him for His goodness and mercy (Psalm 100:4).

74. In Christ, I rejoice in His presence, finding peace and joy in His Holy Spirit (Psalm 16:9).

75. In Christ, I trust in His unfailing love, knowing He is my rock and my salvation (Psalm 62:2).

76. In Christ, I take refuge in Him, finding strength and security in His mighty hand (Psalm 46:1).

77. In Christ, I seek His face continually, longing to dwell in His presence forever (Psalm 27:4).

78. In Christ, I rejoice in His salvation, singing praises to Him, my strength and my song (Psalm 118:14).

79. In Christ, I trust in His unfailing love, knowing He is my refuge and my fortress (Psalm 91:2).

80. In Christ, I lift up my soul to Him, seeking His guidance and direction in all things (Psalm 25:1).

81. In Christ, I give thanks to the Lord, for He is good, and His love endures forever (Psalm 107:1).

82. In Christ, I praise Him with all my heart, declaring His wonders and His glory (Psalm 9:1).

83. In Christ, I sing praises to His name, exalting Him above all gods (Psalm 95:2).

84. In Christ, I trust in His unfailing love, knowing He is my rock and my salvation (Psalm 62:7).

85. In Christ, I rejoice in His presence, finding strength and joy in His Holy Spirit (Psalm 16:11).

86. In Christ, I take refuge in Him, knowing He is my shield and my fortress (Psalm 18:2).

87. In Christ, I seek His face earnestly, longing to dwell in His

presence forever (Psalm 27:8).

88. In Christ, I rejoice in His salvation, singing praises to Him, my strength and my song (Psalm 118:21).

89. In Christ, I trust in His unfailing love, knowing He is my refuge and my strength (Psalm 59:16).

90. In Christ, I praise Him with a grateful heart, giving thanks to Him for His goodness and mercy (Psalm 100:4).

91. In Christ, I rejoice in His presence, finding peace and joy in His Holy Spirit (Psalm 16:9).

92. In Christ, I trust in His unfailing love, knowing He is my rock and my salvation (Psalm 62:2).

93. In Christ, I take refuge in Him, finding strength and security in His mighty hand (Psalm 46:1).

94. In Christ, I seek His face continually, longing to dwell in His presence forever (Psalm 27:4).

95. In Christ, I rejoice in His salvation, singing praises to Him, my strength and my song (Psalm 118:14).

96. In Christ, I trust in His unfailing love, knowing He is my refuge and my fortress (Psalm 91:2).

97. In Christ, I lift up my soul to Him, seeking His guidance and direction in all things (Psalm 25:1).

98. In Christ, I give thanks to the Lord, for He is good, and His love endures forever (Psalm 107:1).

99. In Christ, I praise Him with all my heart, declaring His wonders and His glory (Psalm 9:1).

100. In Christ, I sing praises to His name, exalting Him above all gods (Psalm 95:2).

May these prayers based on Psalms enrich your spiritual journey and deepen your relationship with Christ.

100 prayer points inspired by the prophetic books from Daniel to Malachi:

1. In Christ, I acknowledge Your sovereignty, O Lord, just as Daniel did, recognizing that You alone are the true King of kings and Lord of lords (Daniel 2:20-23).

2. In Christ, I seek Your wisdom and understanding, O God, just as Daniel did, knowing that You are the revealer of mysteries and the source of all knowledge (Daniel 2:21).

3. In Christ, I humble myself before You, O Lord, just as Daniel did, confessing my sins and the sins of my people, seeking Your mercy and forgiveness (Daniel 9:4-19).

4. In Christ, I stand firm in my faith, just as Shadrach, Meshach, and Abednego did, trusting in You alone, even in the face of adversity and persecution (Daniel 3:17-18).

5. In Christ, I rely on Your protection, O God, just as Daniel did, knowing that You are my refuge and my fortress, shielding me from harm (Daniel 6:22).

6. In Christ, I declare Your righteousness and faithfulness, O Lord, just as the prophet Micah did, proclaiming Your justice and mercy to all generations (Micah 6:8).

7. In Christ, I repent of my sins and turn to You, O God, just as the people of Judah did, seeking Your forgiveness and restoration (Jeremiah 3:22).

8. In Christ, I intercede for my nation and its leaders, just as Daniel did, lifting up prayers and supplications on behalf of my people (Daniel 9:20-21).

9. In Christ, I long for Your presence and Your glory, O Lord, just as the psalmist did, thirsting for You in a dry

and weary land (Psalm 63:1).

10. In Christ, I await Your coming kingdom, O God, just as the prophets foretold, eagerly anticipating the day when You will reign over all the earth (Zechariah 14:9).

11. In Christ, I praise You for Your faithfulness, O Lord, just as the prophet Habakkuk did, rejoicing in Your salvation and Your mighty deeds (Habakkuk 3:17-19).

12. In Christ, I cry out to You in times of trouble, O God, just as the prophet Jeremiah did, seeking Your deliverance and Your peace (Jeremiah 33:3).

13. In Christ, I lift up my voice in worship and adoration, just as the psalmists did, magnifying Your holy name and exalting Your majesty (Psalm 145:1-3).

14. In Christ, I put my hope in Your promises, O Lord, just as the prophet Isaiah did, trusting in Your word and Your unfailing love (Isaiah 40:31).

15. In Christ, I proclaim Your righteousness and Your salvation, O God, just as the prophet Isaiah did, declaring Your glory among the nations (Isaiah 52:7).

16. In Christ, I seek Your guidance and Your direction, just as the prophet Ezekiel did, listening for Your voice and obeying Your commands (Ezekiel 1:1).

17. In Christ, I confess my sins and the sins of my people, O Lord, just as Daniel did, acknowledging our transgressions and seeking Your mercy (Daniel 9:20).

18. In Christ, I rejoice in Your unfailing love and Your faithfulness, O God, just as the psalmists did, singing praises to Your name forever (Psalm 89:1-2).

19. In Christ, I pray for the restoration of Your people and Your land, just as the prophets did, longing for the day

when You will gather us together again (Jeremiah 29:14).

20. In Christ, I surrender my life to Your will, O Lord, just as the prophet Jonah did, yielding to Your plans and Your purposes (Jonah 2:9).

21. In Christ, I seek Your face and Your favor, O God, just as the prophet Daniel did, desiring to know You and to walk in Your ways (Daniel 9:3).

22. In Christ, I praise You for Your mercy and Your grace, just as the psalmists did, exalting Your lovingkindness and Your compassion (Psalm 103:1-5).

23. In Christ, I lift up prayers of thanksgiving and gratitude, just as the psalmists did, offering sacrifices of praise to You, O Lord (Psalm 50:14).

24. In Christ, I trust in Your unfailing love and Your provision, just as the prophet Jeremiah did, relying on You for strength and sustenance (Jeremiah 17:7-8).

25. In Christ, I seek Your face and Your presence, O God, just as the prophet Ezekiel did, longing to dwell in Your holy temple (Ezekiel 43:5).

26. In Christ, I pray for the peace of Jerusalem and the salvation of Israel, just as the psalmists did, interceding for Your chosen people (Psalm 122:6).

27. In Christ, I cry out for Your justice and Your righteousness, just as the prophets did, pleading for Your intervention in a world filled with sin and injustice (Isaiah 1:17).

28. In Christ, I rejoice in Your salvation and Your victory, just as the psalmists did, singing praises to You, O Lord, for Your mighty deeds (Psalm 20:5).

29. In Christ, I lift up prayers of supplication and petition,

just as the prophets did, seeking Your mercy and Your guidance (Jeremiah 42:2).

30. In Christ, I confess my sins and the sins of my ancestors, just as the prophets did, acknowledging our transgressions and seeking Your forgiveness (Daniel 9:5).

31. In Christ, I declare Your goodness and Your faithfulness, O Lord, just as the psalmists did, magnifying Your holy name and Your mighty deeds (Psalm 107:1-2).

32. In Christ, I seek Your face and Your favor, just as the prophets did, desiring to know Your will and to walk in Your ways (Jeremiah 29:12).

33. In Christ, I lift up prayers of intercession and supplication, just as the prophets did, standing in the gap for Your people (Jeremiah 7:16).

34. In Christ, I rejoice in Your salvation and Your deliverance, just as the psalmists did, singing praises to Your name forever (Psalm 18:1-3).

35. In Christ, I trust in Your unfailing love and Your provision, just as the prophets did, relying on You for strength and sustenance (Isaiah 40:31).

36. In Christ, I praise You for Your mercy and Your grace, just as the psalmists did, exalting Your lovingkindness and Your compassion (Psalm 86:5).

37. In Christ, I seek Your guidance and Your direction, just as the prophets did, listening for Your voice and obeying Your commands (Isaiah 30:21).

38. In Christ, I confess my sins and the sins of my people, just as the prophets did, acknowledging our transgressions and seeking Your forgiveness (Daniel 9:20).

39. In Christ, I declare Your righteousness and Your

faithfulness, just as the psalmists did, proclaiming Your justice and Your mercy to all generations (Psalm 36:5-6).

40. In Christ, I lift up prayers of thanksgiving and praise, just as the psalmists did, offering sacrifices of praise to You, O Lord (Psalm 95:1-2).

41. In Christ, I seek Your face and Your favor, just as the prophets did, desiring to know You and to walk in Your ways (Jeremiah 7:23).

42. In Christ, I rejoice in Your salvation and Your victory, just as the psalmists did, singing praises to You, O Lord, for Your mighty deeds (Psalm 9:1-2).

43. In Christ, I lift up prayers of intercession and supplication, just as the prophets did, standing in the gap for Your people (Jeremiah 14:11-12).

44. In Christ, I confess my sins and the sins of my ancestors, just as the prophets did, acknowledging our transgressions and seeking Your forgiveness (Daniel 9:8).

45. In Christ, I declare Your goodness and Your faithfulness, O Lord, just as the psalmists did, magnifying Your holy name and Your mighty deeds (Psalm 119:68).

46. In Christ, I seek Your face and Your favor, just as the prophets did, desiring to know Your will and to walk in Your ways (Isaiah 1:19).

47. In Christ, I lift up prayers of intercession and supplication, just as the prophets did, standing in the gap for Your people (Jeremiah 29:7).

48. In Christ, I rejoice in Your salvation and Your deliverance, just as the psalmists did, singing praises to Your name forever (Psalm 40:16).

49. In Christ, I trust in Your unfailing love and Your

provision, just as the prophets did, relying on You for strength and sustenance (Isaiah 58:11).

50. In Christ, I praise You for Your mercy and Your grace, just as the psalmists did, exalting Your lovingkindness and Your compassion (Psalm 103:8).

51. In Christ, I seek Your guidance and Your direction, just as the prophets did, listening for Your voice and obeying Your commands (Jeremiah 42:3).

52. In Christ, I confess my sins and the sins of my people, just as the prophets did, acknowledging our transgressions and seeking Your forgiveness (Daniel 9:20).

53. In Christ, I declare Your righteousness and Your faithfulness, just as the psalmists did, proclaiming Your justice and Your mercy to all generations (Psalm 145:17).

54. In Christ, I lift up prayers of thanksgiving and praise, just as the psalmists did, offering sacrifices of praise to You, O Lord (Psalm 136:1-3).

55. In Christ, I seek Your face and Your favor, just as the prophets did, desiring to know You and to walk in Your ways (Jeremiah 29:13).

56. In Christ, I rejoice in Your salvation and Your victory, just as the psalmists did, singing praises to You, O Lord, for Your mighty deeds (Psalm 28:6-7).

57. In Christ, I lift up prayers of intercession and supplication, just as the prophets did, standing in the gap for Your people (Jeremiah 7:16).

58. In Christ, I confess my sins and the sins of my ancestors, just as the prophets did, acknowledging our transgressions and seeking Your forgiveness (Daniel 9:9).

59. In Christ, I declare Your goodness and Your faithfulness,

O Lord, just as the psalmists did, magnifying Your holy name and Your mighty deeds (Psalm 107:8-9).

60. In Christ, I seek Your face and Your favor, just as the prophets did, desiring to know Your will and to walk in Your ways (Jeremiah 6:16).

61. In Christ, I lift up prayers of intercession and supplication, just as the prophets did, standing in the gap for Your people (Jeremiah 18:20).

62. In Christ, I rejoice in Your salvation and Your deliverance, just as the psalmists did, singing praises to Your name forever (Psalm 13:5-6).

63. In Christ, I trust in Your unfailing love and Your provision, just as the prophets did, relying on You for strength and sustenance (Isaiah 26:3-4).

64. In Christ, I praise You for Your mercy and Your grace, just as the psalmists did, exalting Your lovingkindness and Your compassion (Psalm 36:7-9).

65. In Christ, I seek Your guidance and Your direction, just as the prophets did, listening for Your voice and obeying Your commands (Jeremiah 7:23).

66. In Christ, I confess my sins and the sins of my people, just as the prophets did, acknowledging our transgressions and seeking Your forgiveness (Daniel 9:20).

67. In Christ, I declare Your righteousness and Your faithfulness, just as the psalmists did, proclaiming Your justice and Your mercy to all generations (Psalm 111:7-9).

68. In Christ, I lift up prayers of thanksgiving and praise, just as the psalmists did, offering sacrifices of praise to You, O Lord (Psalm 95:1-3).

69. In Christ, I seek Your face and Your favor, just as the

prophets did, desiring to know You and to walk in Your ways (Jeremiah 33:3).

70. In Christ, I rejoice in Your salvation and Your victory, just as the psalmists did, singing praises to You, O Lord, for Your mighty deeds (Psalm 20:5-6).

71. In Christ, I lift up prayers of intercession and supplication, just as the prophets did, standing in the gap for Your people (Jeremiah 7:16).

72. In Christ, I confess my sins and the sins of my ancestors, just as the prophets did, acknowledging our transgressions and seeking Your forgiveness (Daniel 9:9).

73. In Christ, I declare Your goodness and Your faithfulness, O Lord, just as the psalmists did, magnifying Your holy name and Your mighty deeds (Psalm 40:10-11).

74. In Christ, I seek Your face and Your favor, just as the prophets did, desiring to know Your will and to walk in Your ways (Isaiah 65:24).

75. In Christ, I lift up prayers of intercession and supplication, just as the prophets did, standing in the gap for Your people (Jeremiah 14:11-12).

76. In Christ, I rejoice in Your salvation and Your deliverance, just as the psalmists did, singing praises to Your name forever (Psalm 28:6-7).

77. In Christ, I trust in Your unfailing love and Your provision, just as the prophets did, relying on You for strength and sustenance (Isaiah 30:15).

78. In Christ, I praise You for Your mercy and Your grace, just as the psalmists did, exalting Your lovingkindness and Your compassion (Psalm 36:5-6).

79. In Christ, I seek Your guidance and Your direction, just

as the prophets did, listening for Your voice and obeying Your commands (Jeremiah 42:4).

80. In Christ, I confess my sins and the sins of my people, just as the prophets did, acknowledging our transgressions and seeking Your forgiveness (Daniel 9:20).

81. In Christ, I declare Your righteousness and Your faithfulness, just as the psalmists did, proclaiming Your justice and Your mercy to all generations (Psalm 145:17-19).

82. In Christ, I lift up prayers of thanksgiving and praise, just as the psalmists did, offering sacrifices of praise to You, O Lord (Psalm 100:1-5).

83. In Christ, I seek Your face and Your favor, just as the prophets did, desiring to know You and to walk in Your ways (Jeremiah 17:7-8).

84. In Christ, I rejoice in Your salvation and Your victory, just as the psalmists did, singing praises to You, O Lord, for Your mighty deeds (Psalm 21:1-2).

85. In Christ, I lift up prayers of intercession and supplication, just as the prophets did, standing in the gap for Your people (Jeremiah 29:7).

86. In Christ, I confess my sins and the sins of my ancestors, just as the prophets did, acknowledging our transgressions and seeking Your forgiveness (Daniel 9:8).

87. In Christ, I declare Your goodness and Your faithfulness, O Lord, just as the psalmists did, magnifying Your holy name and Your mighty deeds (Psalm 86:5-7).

88. In Christ, I seek Your face and Your favor, just as the prophets did, desiring to know Your will and to walk in Your ways (Jeremiah 6:16).

89. In Christ, I lift up prayers of intercession and supplication, just as the prophets did, standing in the gap for Your people (Jeremiah 18:20).

90. In Christ, I rejoice in Your salvation and Your deliverance, just as the psalmists did, singing praises to Your name forever (Psalm 13:5-6).

91. In Christ, I trust in Your unfailing love and Your provision, just as the prophets did, relying on You for strength and sustenance (Isaiah 26:3-4).

92. In Christ, I praise You for Your mercy and Your grace, just as the psalmists did, exalting Your lovingkindness and Your compassion (Psalm 36:7-9).

93. In Christ, I seek Your guidance and Your direction, just as the prophets did, listening for Your voice and obeying Your commands (Jeremiah 7:23).

94. In Christ, I confess my sins and the sins of my people, just as the prophets did, acknowledging our transgressions and seeking Your forgiveness (Daniel 9:20).

95. In Christ, I declare Your righteousness and Your faithfulness, just as the psalmists did, proclaiming Your justice and Your mercy to all generations (Psalm 145:17-19).

96. In Christ, I lift up prayers of thanksgiving and praise, just as the psalmists did, offering sacrifices of praise to You, O Lord (Psalm 100:1-5).

97. In Christ, I seek Your face and Your favor, just as the prophets did, desiring to know You and to walk in Your ways (Jeremiah 17:7-8).

98. In Christ, I rejoice in Your salvation and Your victory, just as the psalmists did, singing praises to You, O Lord, for

Your mighty deeds (Psalm 21:1-2).

99. In Christ, I lift up prayers of intercession and supplication, just as the prophets did, standing in the gap for Your people (Jeremiah 29:7).

100. In Christ, I confess my sins and the sins of my ancestors, just as the prophets did, acknowledging our transgressions and seeking Your forgiveness (Daniel 9:8).

May these prayers based on the prophetic books inspire and enrich your spiritual journey, drawing you closer to God and His purposes for your life.

In Christ 100 prayer points based on the New Testament.

1. In Christ, I am chosen and predestined to be holy and blameless before God. (Ephesians 1:4)
2. In Christ, I am a beloved child of God, lavished with His great love. (1 John 3:1)
3. In Christ, I am a new creation; the old has passed away, and the new has come. (2 Corinthians 5:17)
4. In Christ, I am an heir of God and a co-heir with Christ, sharing in His glory. (Romans 8:17)
5. In Christ, I am part of a chosen people, a royal priesthood, and a holy nation. (1 Peter 2:9)
6. In Christ, I am washed, sanctified, and justified by the blood of Jesus. (1 Corinthians 6:11)
7. In Christ, nothing can separate me from the love of God. (Romans 8:38-39)
8. In Christ, I am fearfully and wonderfully made, a masterpiece of God's creation. (Psalm 139:14)
9. In Christ, I have redemption and the forgiveness of sins. (Colossians 1:13-14)
10. In Christ, I am crucified with Him, and I now live by faith in His sacrificial love. (Galatians 2:20)
11. In Christ, I am an ambassador for His kingdom, proclaiming His message of reconciliation. (2 Corinthians 5:20)
12. In Christ, I am seated with Him in heavenly places, far above all powers and authorities. (Ephesians 2:6)
13. In Christ, I am set free from the bondage of sin and

empowered to walk in righteousness. (Galatians 5:1)

14. In Christ, I am more than a conqueror through Him who loves me. (Romans 8:37)

15. In Christ, I am transformed by the renewing of my mind, reflecting His image. (Romans 12:2)

16. In Christ, I am hidden with Him, secure in His love and protection. (Colossians 3:3)

17. In Christ, my body is a temple of the Holy Spirit, and I honor God with it. (1 Corinthians 6:19-20)

18. In Christ, I overcome the world by faith, walking in victory and confidence. (1 John 5:4)

19. In Christ, I am filled with power by the Holy Spirit to be His witness to the ends of the earth. (Acts 1:8)

20. In Christ, I present myself as an instrument of righteousness, pleasing to God. (Romans 6:13)

21. In Christ, I am purified and made holy, reflecting His righteousness. (Titus 2:14)

22. In Christ, I am accepted and included in His family, a fellow citizen of His kingdom. (Ephesians 2:19)

23. In Christ, I have abundant life, overflowing with His love, joy, and peace. (John 10:10)

24. In Christ, I am being renewed in knowledge, becoming more like Him day by day. (Colossians 3:10)

25. In Christ, I am called to be holy as He is holy, set apart for His purposes. (1 Peter 1:15-16)

26. In Christ, I am blessed with every spiritual blessing in the heavenly realms. (Ephesians 1:3)

27. In Christ, I am saved and called to live a holy life according to His purpose and grace. (2 Timothy 1:9)

28. In Christ, I am filled with hope and joy, trusting in His

promises for my future. (Romans 15:13)

29. In Christ, I am clothed with His righteousness and identified as His own. (Galatians 3:27)

30. In Christ, I am destined for glory, sharing in His divine nature and inheritance. (2 Peter 1:4)

31. In Christ, I am the apple of God's eye, protected and cherished by Him. (Zechariah 2:8)

32. In Christ, I am restored, strengthened, and established by His grace. (1 Peter 5:10)

33. In Christ, I shine as a light in the world, reflecting His love and truth. (Matthew 5:14)

34. In Christ, I hunger and thirst for righteousness, finding fulfillment in Him. (Matthew 5:6)

35. In Christ, I desire to know Him more deeply, sharing in His sufferings and resurrection power. (Philippians 3:10)

36. In Christ, I seek first His kingdom and righteousness, finding true satisfaction and purpose. (Matthew 6:33)

37. In Christ, I am a member of His body, united with other believers in love and fellowship. (1 Corinthians 12:27)

38. In Christ, I have access to the wisdom of God and the mind of Christ. (1 Corinthians 2:16)

39. In Christ, I bear the fruit of the Spirit, displaying His love, joy, peace, and more. (Galatians 5:22-23)

40. In Christ, I am sealed with the Holy Spirit, guaranteed of my inheritance and salvation. (Ephesians 1:13-14)

41. In Christ, I am rooted and established in His love, filled with His fullness. (Ephesians 3:17-19)

42. In Christ, I eagerly await His return, knowing that I will be like Him when He appears. (1 John 3:2)

43. In Christ, I walk by the Spirit, overcoming the desires of

the flesh and living in freedom. (Galatians 5:16)

44. In Christ, I am justified and sanctified, made righteous and set apart for His purposes. (Romans 5:1)

45. In Christ, I am reconciled to God and entrusted with the ministry of reconciliation. (2 Corinthians 5:18)

46. In Christ, I am empowered to stand firm against the schemes of the enemy, wielding the armor of God. (Ephesians 6:10-18)

47. In Christ, I am filled with the peace of God, ruling in my heart and mind. (Philippians 4:7)

48. In Christ, I offer myself as a living sacrifice, holy and pleasing to God. (Romans 12:1)

49. In Christ, I am more than a conqueror, facing trials and tribulations with His strength and courage. (Romans 8:37)

50. In Christ, I am rooted and built up in Him, strengthened in my faith and overflowing with thankfulness. (Colossians 2:7)

51. In Christ, I am seated with Him in heavenly places, reigning with Him in authority and power. (Ephesians 2:6)

52. In Christ, I am confident of His plans and purposes for my life, knowing that He works all things for my good. (Jeremiah 29:11)

53. In Christ, I am filled with the knowledge of His will, walking in wisdom and understanding. (Colossians 1:9)

54. In Christ, I am rooted in love, grounded in His truth, and filled with His Spirit. (Ephesians 3:17)

55. In Christ, I am a vessel of His grace and a witness of His love to the world. (Acts 1:8)

56. In Christ, I am strengthened with power through His Spirit, able to do all things through Him who gives me strength. (Philippians 4:13)

57. In Christ, I am empowered to love others as He has loved me, bearing His image and reflecting His character. (John 13:34-35)

58. In Christ, I am forgiven of all my sins, washed clean by His precious blood. (Ephesians 1:7)

59. In Christ, I am called to walk in humility and gentleness, bearing with one another in love. (Ephesians 4:2)

60. In Christ, I am filled with hope and joy, anchored in the promises of His word. (Romans 15:13)

61. In Christ, I am anointed by His Spirit, equipped and empowered to fulfill His purposes. (1 John 2:27)

62. In Christ, I am called to live a life worthy of the calling I have received, bearing fruit in every good work. (Colossians 1:10)

63. In Christ, I am surrounded by His peace, guarding my heart and mind in Him. (Philippians 4:7)

64. In Christ, I am secure in His love, confident that nothing can separate me from His presence. (Romans 8:38-39)

65. In Christ, I am victorious over every trial and temptation, standing firm in His promises. (1 Corinthians 15:57)

66. In Christ, I am filled with the joy of the Lord, rejoicing in His salvation and goodness. (Psalm 16:11)

67. In Christ, I am called to walk in unity with fellow believers, bearing with one another in love. (Ephesians 4:3)

68. In Christ, I am a living stone, chosen and precious in God's sight, built into a spiritual house. (1 Peter 2:4-5)

69. In Christ, I am strengthened with power through His Spirit, able to endure and persevere through all things. (Ephesians 3:16)

70. In Christ, I am a temple of the Holy Spirit, set apart for His glory and filled with His presence. (1 Corinthians 6:19-20)

71. In Christ, I am called to walk in humility and gentleness, bearing with one another in love. (Ephesians 4:2)

72. In Christ, I am filled with faith, trusting in His promises and believing for His miracles. (Hebrews 11:1)

73. In Christ, I am rooted and grounded in love, rooted in His truth and grounded in His grace. (Ephesians 3:17)

74. In Christ, I am a chosen people, a royal priesthood, a holy nation, God's special possession. (1 Peter 2:9)

75. In Christ, I am a co-heir with Christ, sharing in His inheritance and glory. (Romans 8:17)

76. In Christ, I am called to bear fruit, producing a harvest of righteousness and love. (John 15:5)

77. In Christ, I am filled with the fruit of the Spirit, walking in love, joy, peace, patience, kindness, goodness, faithfulness, gentleness, and self-control. (Galatians 5:22-23)

78. In Christ, I am seated with Him in heavenly places, far above all rule and authority, power and dominion. (Ephesians 1:20-21)

79. In Christ, I am redeemed and forgiven, set free from the power of sin and death. (Ephesians 1:7)

80. In Christ, I am called to be a light in the world, shining His love and truth to those around me. (Matthew 5:14)

81. In Christ, I am empowered to overcome every obstacle and challenge, victorious through His strength.

(Philippians 4:13)

82. In Christ, I am filled with His peace, a peace that surpasses all understanding and guards my heart and mind. (Philippians 4:7)

83. In Christ, I am blessed with every spiritual blessing in the heavenly realms, chosen and adopted as His child. (Ephesians 1:3)

84. In Christ, I am called to walk in love, imitating His sacrificial love and extending grace to others. (Ephesians 5:1-2)

85. In Christ, I am empowered to live a life of purity and holiness, set apart for His purposes. (1 Thessalonians 4:7)

86. In Christ, I am an overcomer, conquering every trial and temptation through His strength. (Romans 8:37)

87. In Christ, I am called to walk in humility and gentleness, bearing with one another in love. (Ephesians 4:2)

88. In Christ, I am filled with His joy, rejoicing in His salvation and goodness. (Philippians 4:4)

89. In Christ, I am a vessel of His grace, filled with His Spirit and empowered to live for His glory. (2 Timothy 2:21)

90. In Christ, I am called to walk in obedience to His word, living a life that honors and pleases Him. (Colossians 3:16)

91. In Christ, I am called to be a witness of His love and truth, proclaiming His gospel to the ends of the earth. (Acts 1:8)

92. In Christ, I am called to walk in faith, trusting in His promises and believing for His miracles. (Hebrews 11:6)

93. In Christ, I am strengthened with power through His Spirit, able to endure and persevere through all things. (Ephesians 3:16)

94. In Christ, I am called to walk in unity with fellow believers, bearing with one another in love. (Ephesians 4:3)

95. In Christ, I am a chosen people, a royal priesthood, a holy nation, God's special possession. (1 Peter 2:9)

96. In Christ, I am a co-heir with Christ, sharing in His inheritance and glory. (Romans 8:17)

97. In Christ, I am called to bear fruit, producing a harvest of righteousness and love. (John 15:5)

98. In Christ, I am filled with the fruit of the Spirit, walking in love, joy, peace, patience, kindness, goodness, faithfulness, gentleness, and self-control. (Galatians 5:22-23)

99. In Christ, I am seated with Him in heavenly places, far above all rule and authority, power and dominion. (Ephesians 1:20-21)

100. In Christ, I am redeemed and forgiven, set free from the power of sin and death. (Ephesians 1:7).

Don't miss out!

Visit the website below and you can sign up to receive emails whenever Johannes Tefo publishes a new book. There's no charge and no obligation.

https://books2read.com/r/B-A-UEZX-CQZXC

BOOKS 2 READ

Connecting independent readers to independent writers.

Did you love *Identity In Christ*? Then you should read *Michael For Warfare*[1] by Johannes Tefo!

In the midst of a world plagued by darkness and evil, a powerful ally stands ready to guide and protect us through the turbulent times ahead. "Michael For Warfare" is a compelling and illuminating exploration of how we can partner with the mighty Archangel Michael in the ultimate battle against malevolent forces, heralding the End Time Move of God.

This captivating book delves into the age-old concept of divine warriors and their pivotal role in the cosmic struggle between good and evil. Author Johannes Tefo offers a unique perspective on

---

1. https://books2read.com/u/ml6GRZ

2. https://books2read.com/u/ml6GRZ

Archangel Michael, one of the most renowned celestial warriors, and how we can tap into his divine energy to stand against the rising tide of darkness.

Within these pages, you will embark on a spiritual journey that unveils the secrets of invoking Archangel Michael's protection and guidance. Drawing from ancient texts, mystical traditions, and modern insights, you'll learn how to forge a powerful connection with this benevolent warrior-angel, strengthening your resolve and courage as you face the challenges of our troubled world.

"Michael For Warfare" is a beacon of hope, offering practical advice, heartfelt anecdotes, and inspiring stories that demonstrate the transformative power of aligning with Archangel Michael. As you read this remarkable book, you will discover the tools and knowledge you need to help usher in the End Time Move of God, joining the forces of light to defeat the darkness that threatens our world.

Prepare yourself for a spiritual awakening and be part of a divine alliance that will bring about profound change in the face of adversity. Embrace the wisdom and might of Archangel Michael, and step boldly into the epic battle against evil forces.

Also by Johannes Tefo

Family spiritual Warfare Books
Youth's Guide To Spiritual Warfare
A Women's Guide To Spiritual Warfare

Standalone
Deliver Your Soul From Evil: Self Deliverance Guide
Deliverance From Mind Control: Be Free And Delivered From Every Marine Demons Of Mind Control
Overcoming Spirit Of Stagnation
The 24: Prophetic Word For This Season 2024 And Beyond
Michael For Warfare
Territorial Spirits: Overcome Evil Strongholds in Your Life And Take Over Your Community With Strategic Warfare And Winning Prayers
Prayers Against Suicide Spirit
Spiritual Warfare When Enough is Enough
Identity In Christ

About the Author

Before he started writing Christian books, Johannes got a graduate degree in Film and Television from university of Johannesburg. After that, just to shake things up, he went to equip himself with religious studies, particularly Christianity, just to have knack about the world beyond the curtains of time. And how this body of Christ has transformed millions of people around the world, not neglecting how sadly the movement has been persecuted from time to time. He now writes full time.

www.ingramcontent.com/pod-product-compliance
Lightning Source LLC
Chambersburg PA
CBHW070545160726
48003CB00005B/1894